PREDATORS

Created and Produced by Firecrest Books Ltd
in association with John Francis/Bernard Thornton Artists

Copyright © 1999 Firecrest Books Ltd
and Copyright © 1999 John Francis/Bernard Thornton Artists

Published by Tangerine Press™, an imprint of Scholastic Inc.
555 Broadway, New York, NY 10012

ISBN 0-439-09590-5

Library of Congress Cataloging-in-Publication Data

Stonehouse, Bernard.
Predators / Bernard Stonehouse ; illustrated by John Francis.
p. cm.
Includes index.
SUMMARY: An introduction to predators on land, in the air, and in
the water, highlighting the amazing range of adaptation employed to
catch, subdue, and consume a living meal.
ISBN 0-439-09590-5 (pbk.)
1. Predatory animals Juvenile literature. [1. Predatory animals.]
I. Francis, John, 1950- ill. II. Title.
QL758 .S75 1999
591.5'3--dc21
99-29318
CIP

Printed and bound in Belgium
First printing September 1999

PREDATORS

Bernard Stonehouse

Illustrated by
John Francis

TANGERINE PRESS™ and associated logo
and design are trademarks of Scholastic Inc.

For David Francis

Art and Editorial Direction by
Peter Sackett

Designed by
Paul Richards, Designers & Partners

Edited by
Norman Barrett

Color separation by
Job Color, Italy

Printed and bound by
Casterman, Belgium

— Contents —

Introduction	6
Lions	8
Barn owl	10
Hyenas	12
Leopard seal	14
Grizzly bear	16
Komodo dragon	18
Praying mantis	20
Stoat	22
Bird-eating spider	24
Heron	26
Timber wolves	28
Long-eared bat	30
Crocodile	32
Mongoose	34
Bengal tiger	36
Shark	38
Kingfisher	40
Anaconda	42
Freshwater pike	44
African hunting dogs	46
Index	48

Introduction THEY KILL TO LIVE

Every day millions of animals die prematurely, not from enmity or ill-will of man but from the claws and teeth of other animals. Those that die and are eaten are the prey. Those that own the claws and teeth are the predators. Predator-eating-prey is one of the fundamental ways in which energy and nutrients pass from one form of life to another — one of the basic ways in which the world works.

Many of the animals we admire most, for their structure, skill, courage and resourcefulness, and for a host of other qualities we admire in ourselves, are the predators. This book is about predators — how they live and work, and how they are shaped, formed, and equipped to catch and eat other animals.

Its objective? Not to horrify, not to linger over the less pleasant aspects of animal life, not to glory in predation — certainly not to justify man's endless predation on man and other animals.

Both the artist and the writer seek to share, with children and adults alike, their love and respect for animals as they are — not as sentimentalists present them. Predators, just as much as prey, have a living to make. Like most other animals, they take what they need from the world — but no more. They kill only to live.

Cheetah: speedy predator of the African savanna.

Lions POWERFUL HUNTERS OF THE SAVANNA

These two female lions, attacking a herd of African buffaloes, have singled out an old bull and are trying to bring him down. He is bigger than they are and still a powerful animal that can roll, kick with his hooves, and butt with his horns. But these are experienced lions that know how to attack a buffalo. They have done it many times before. One threatens from the front, while the second grabs the bull around the neck and hangs on with teeth and razor-sharp claws. Eventually one or the other will grab his throat to stop him breathing, and that will be the end of the bull.

Others from the herd may come to help the buffalo by charging and knocking the lions off, but that does not often happen. If there are calves among them, they try to protect those instead of the old ones. Within a few minutes the herd will have moved off, forgetting about the bull. They will be grazing peacefully, while the rest of the lions — including the cubs — gather around to enjoy their supper.

A family group of lions, called a "pride," usually includes a single large male and two or three females with their cubs.

Barn owl SILENT HUNTER OF THE NIGHT

Pale, shy birds of forests and woodland edges, barn owls hunt in the half-light of evenings and early morning, when their black, staring eyes, set in a mask of stiff white feathers, see everything sharply. Even sharper are their ears, invisible under the head feathers but tuned acutely to hear the faintest rustle among leaves and undergrowth.

During the day, barn owls roost invisibly in trees, in caverns or hollows on cliff faces, and in lofts of barns and churches, where they also build their nests. You are most likely to see them toward sunset as the world darkens and their prey become active. They hunt a wide variety of small animals, including birds, insects, mice, voles, and young rabbits.

Long wings and soft, downy feathers give barn owls a silent, ghostly flight. Swooping and gliding low over the ground, they perch on stump or fence post to watch and listen. Then they pounce, dropping noiselessly and grasping their prey with long, curved talons. A quick bite to crush the skull and away they fly to pull their victim to pieces, perhaps to feed it to three or four downy young in the nest. Then back to hunt they go again, through the dark of night, when hearing becomes even more important, to the first light of morning.

The barn owl's skull shows a long, powerful bill, deep-set eye sockets, and large ear openings behind the eyes.

Eight sharp, curved talons
(claws) are ready to close as
the owl strikes at its prey.

Hyenas PACK-HUNTERS OF THE AFRICAN PLAINS

Like rough, woolly dogs, these spotted hyenas are part of a pack of fifteen that hunt together on the African plains. These three are young ones, born last year and still growing. Though surrounded by antelopes, zebras, young giraffes, and other likely prey, they are not strong enough and cannot run fast enough to hunt on their own. So instead they hunt with older animals, learning as they go along.

During the day they keep out of the hot sun, sheltering in caves and under shrubs. The packs form in the evening and hunt into the night. Fifteen or twenty hyenas working together can surround a group of antelopes and confuse them, then single out and kill one or perhaps two of the weaker ones. This time they have caught an antelope. After the older ones have fed, there may not be much left for the young hyenas. But their powerful jaws can rip through skin and chomp bones so they will finish every scrap.

Together, hyenas can attack a lion or cheetah and rob it of its prey.

Leopard seal THE PENGUIN'S DEADLY ENEMY

A leopard seal tries its best to grab a sleek, fat gentoo penguin, while the penguin twists and turns to keep out of reach. They are both excellent swimmers. The penguin can probably swim faster than the seal over short distances, changing speed and direction and diving more freely. The seal has more staying power and after a few minutes can tire the penguin out. Both have to come to the surface to breathe, and that is where the penguin is most likely to be taken. If the penguin is caught, the seal will crush it in its powerful jaws, beat its body against the surface of the sea to skin it, then swallow the carcass. The skin and feathers float away, and the predator swims off in search of its next meal.

Seals are warm-blooded mammals, penguins are warm-blooded birds, and both live in the cold waters of the Southern Ocean. Many kinds of seals live on squid, fish, and shrimps, but leopard seals — so-called because they are spotted, as well as being fierce hunters — prey particularly on penguins.

A leopard seal can be up to 10 ft (3 m) long and weigh as much as 600 lb (270 kg). A gentoo penguin is about 30 in (75 cm) long and weighs around 13 lb (6 kg). It takes five or six penguins to make a square meal for the seal.

Grizzly bear FEASTING ON FISH

This grizzly bear is fishing in a fast-flowing stream and has caught a fat, lively salmon. He will probably catch another thirty or forty today, and the same number tomorrow and every day for the few weeks that the salmon are plentiful. If he is big, smaller bears will keep away. If he is a small bear, he may have to fight to keep others off his stretch of river.

Grizzlies are huge brown bears of North American forests. If you see two or three together, they are most probably a mother with young cubs. Adults without cubs usually wander alone, keeping out of each other's way. Most times there is not a lot of food in the forest, so it is best for them to stay apart.

There is hardly anything to eat in winter, so grizzlies sleep from October to February or March. In spring they awake thin and hungry to feed mainly on young shoots of shrubs and trees. They eat eggs from birds' nests, and birds, mice, squirrels, and other small mammals they can catch and any dead animals they find. They love wild honey scraped from tree nests.

Salmon become the main food in autumn, when they swim in thousands up the rivers to breed. The bears are hungry, but this is also the time when they need to fatten for their winter sleep.

Huge forepaws with five strong claws scoop the fish from the water.

Grizzly bears are usually hungry and on the lookout for a meal.

Komodo dragon FIERCE FOREST LIZARD

Dragons are fairy tale beasts that roar and spit fire. This is not a storybook dragon — just a very big lizard, 10 ft (3 m) long or more, that grunts and flicks its forked tongue as it roams through the forest. It lives on Komodo, one of the Lesser Sunda Islands of Indonesia, and on two or three neighboring islands. There are only a few dozen of them left in the world. When young, they are slim and fast-moving. They have to be, because older adults of the same species will catch and eat them if they can. In later life, when they are ten to twelve years old, they begin to grow fat, clumsy, and slower.

You may wonder how this one could hope to catch such a lively, agile monkey as a macaque. In the early morning, like all other reptiles, it is cold and slow-moving. It finds a comfortable place at the forest edge and lies very still, soaking up the early morning sunshine. The macaque, young and inquisitive, wants to know what this strange-looking heap is all about. It swings down from the trees, coming closer and closer, and puts out a paw to feel the creature. That is when the predator comes to life, rearing up with tail lashing, teeth and claws grabbing.

A big Komodo dragon can swallow a small monkey in one gulp or tear one this size to pieces without any difficulty. This macaque may be lucky. It seems to have gotten away, but only just. It will certainly remember — next time it sees a sleepy-looking Komodo dragon, it will keep its distance.

Praying mantis SILENT STALKER

The locust below, a kind of grasshopper, is feeding busily on grass, grasping it with those long forelegs and stuffing it into the jaws beneath its head. Despite its large compound eyes, it has not yet spotted the mantis moving silently into position behind. The mantis does, after all, look remarkably like a stick or complex blade of grass.

But the mantis has seen the locust and is poised ready to pounce. Its body can shoot forward in a moment, the forelimbs folding like a penknife over the locust, with spines ready to grasp and hold. The pincers in front of its head will move into action, and the jaws of the mantis are ready to bite.

The locust, however, is a master of rapid escape and has not yet lost the game. We do not know what it sees with those massive eyes, but we know that they detect very slight movement. The locust has probably registered the presence of the mantis but not yet been triggered into activity. When that happens, powerful internal muscles in its long, folded legs will snap them straight in an instant, catapulting the locust over 6 ft (2 m) into the air. That puts it well beyond the reach of the mantis, who will have to stalk another locust.

Stoat HOW TO CATCH A RABBIT

Here is a rabbit — quite a big one — about to be attacked by a stoat. It is very likely to die. Stoats are major enemies of rabbits, and when the two meet, the stoat nearly always wins.

This is surprising, because stoats are relatively small. They are slim, fierce mammals, related to weasels, ferrets, polecats, and badgers. They have strong jaws and a taste for other small mammals. But a big male stoat weighs only about 1 lb (450 g), no more than a fairly small rabbit. A large, fully grown rabbit can be three to five times as heavy.

Rabbits eat grass, leaves, shoots, and other vegetable materials. Though pet rabbits are gentle creatures that like being stroked and do not usually bite, wild rabbits can be quite fierce. They fight among themselves for living space, using their teeth and strong hind legs. A large wild rabbit can defend itself fiercely if attacked by a cat or a rat. But large or small, rabbits are very much in danger if a stoat is about. The stoat, weaving through the grass, sitting up to make its presence known, chattering and squeaking through its teeth, seems to terrify the rabbit on sight and take away its ability either to defend itself or to run.

The stoat comes closer, pouncing on the rabbit and sinking its teeth into the furry neck. Usually the rabbit dies immediately without a struggle, and the stoat eats well for the next few days until only the skin remains.

A stoat attacking a rabbit seems first to terrify it, so the rabbit can neither run nor fight.

Bird-eating spider HAIRY MONSTER

Here is something from a nightmare — a black monster with sharp, pointed fangs and eight hairy legs. Fortunately for us it is smaller than it looks — only about 7 in (18 cm) across. An adult specimen would fit comfortably onto a large saucer. But you still would not want to find it in your bed.

You can tell it is a spider from the eight legs and the four spinnerets on the abdomen that produce silky webbing. Related to the tarantula spiders (which are well known for their poisoned bite), it is called a bird-eating spider because small birds and their eggs are among its prey. It hunts by lying in wait, then running fast, grabbing its prey, and poisoning it with a bite.

The poison of a bird-eating spider
is not fatal to humans, but the fine
black hairs on its legs carry an
irritant that makes human skin
uncomfortably swollen and red.
Wear gloves if you ever have to
handle a bird-eating spider.

Heron LONG-LEGGED FISHERMAN

We are below the surface of a clear, still pool somewhere in Europe. There are green water weeds around us, and the leaf of a waterlily rests on the surface above. Two roach swim by, small silvery fish with yellow-tipped fins that merge quickly into the background. It is early morning, and all is very quiet and peaceful.

Suddenly a face appears — a gray head with two bright, beady eyes and a pointed yellow bill — and darts down quick as a flash. The bill opens and closes around one of the fish. Face and fish disappear together. The ripples settle, the remaining fish scuttles for cover, and all is peaceful again.

The heron — for that is what the face belongs to — straightens up, throws back its bill, and swallows the fish headfirst. Wading in the water, its long legs thin and straight like yellow reed stalks, it moves slowly with head down and shoulders hunched, peering like a shortsighted old fisherman into the pool, scratching the mud with clawed feet, watching carefully for signs of movement.

After catching and swallowing a dozen or more fish, the heron spreads its long, gray wings and takes off heavily, flying back to its nest in the nearby trees. There, three hungry chicks are waiting for breakfast. Perched on the side of the nest, it vomits up the fish one by one, distributing them among the nestlings. It is not an even distribution — the liveliest chick gets most. But even the smallest and quietest gains a small, slippery fish for breakfast and sinks back satisfied into the nest.

Herons make untidy stick nests in tall trees, usually close to the lake or river where they catch their fish.

Timber wolves HUNTING A CARIBOU

Here in the forests of northern Canada stands a bull caribou. He is old and tired, separated from his herd, and about to fight a last battle with his old enemies the timber wolves.

You can tell his sex and age from the size of his antlers and the number of points, or bony "tines," they carry. He has met timber wolves many times before, and has learned how best to deal with them. If he turns and runs, they will run faster and bring him down. He may charge forward, with head down and antlers pointing like spears at his enemies. In this case, the wolves will scatter, for they recognize an old fighter when they see one and cannot afford to be injured by those points. But they are hungry and will gather again in minutes. He may just stand there. So long as he faces them, he is probably safe — until he droops or falls from weariness. Then the wolves will move in.

The wolves see his weakness and draw closer. The one that charges first is the one most likely to be injured — so they wait and watch. Perhaps they will grow tired of waiting and wander off after the herd. But they too probably sense that his time has come, and they may not have to wait long. There will be a token fight, a quick death, a patch of red snow on the forest floor, and the timber wolves will snarl and growl over the remains. The caribou will soon be forgotten, and the wolves will trot off to seek their next meal.

The wolves wait for the caribou to show signs of tiredness or weakness before they move in for the kill.

Long-eared bat HUNTER THAT FLIES BY NIGHT

This long-eared bat has spent its day asleep in a cave, deep in the side of a hill, hanging by its claws from wall or ceiling like a tiny umbrella. Now it is evening. The moon is rising and bats — hundreds of them — have come out to feed. On paper-thin wings, they flutter and swoop through the air, catching beetles, moths, and other flying insects, which they grab and crunch with their sharp little teeth.

Bats are small mammals — some no bigger than mice — warm-blooded and covered with fur. They fly just as well as birds, on wings made of skin stretched tightly between the bones of their fingers, arms, and legs. There is another web of skin between their hindlegs and tail. This makes a kind of basket, where they store some of the insects they catch to eat later. Not all bats have ears as large as these, but all hunt by sound as much as by sight. As they fly past, you can sometimes hear the high-pitched trills and squeaks that they use in hunting. The ears pick up echoes that help them to avoid flying into walls and trees, and to find their prey as well.

Arm bones and finger bones support the extended wings. The hook on the front is a curved thumbnail.

— Crocodile AMBUSHING AN ANTELOPE

Just one second ago this African crocodile was floating like a log on the lake, with only his eyes, nostrils, and brown, scaly back above the surface. The springbok, a kind of antelope, probably saw it but took no notice. It looked just like any other log afloat at the water's edge, and the antelope was thirsty after a day in the hot sun. Now the "log" has sprung into action — a short rush, with jaws open and teeth ready to grab. The springbok has half a second to leap into the air, land just out of reach, and skip away.

If caught, it will be dragged into the water and drowned, and the crocodile will tear it into chunks and eat it. Some chunks may be hidden away for another day. If the antelope gets away, the crocodile will sink back into the water and wait for the next one. With short, stumpy legs, a crocodile has no chance of running an antelope down on land. He can only wait, watch, and keep trying for his supper.

Mongoose AGILE SNAKE HUNTER

The mongoose seems to have an instinctive hatred of snakes. Here a female Indian mongoose, about 3 ft (1 m) long from nose to tip of tail, has found a cobra, a snake more than twice her length. Mongoose and cobra are trying hard to kill each other.

It is an even contest. The mongoose has to grab the cobra by the back of its neck. If she grabs the cobra anywhere else, the cobra has a chance to twist around and bite with its long fangs. If she catches it properly, she will hang on with jaws clamped. But the cobra is quick, with tough, scaly skin and a broad neck that makes it difficult to grab. If the cobra grabs first, the mongoose has thick fur that makes it hard for a bite to penetrate. The mongoose also seems able to resist the snake's poison better than most other animals. But the cobra will jerk as well as bite, beating the mongoose against the ground in an effort to shake it off. The bite and the shaking together would hurt her badly and probably kill her.

A cobra's fangs (front teeth) are linked to poison sacs. One bite could kill a human or other large mammal. But if the cobra turns to slide away, the mongoose will strike.

Bengal tiger FEROCIOUS

Bengal tigers live quiet, lonely lives. Lions hunt on the open plains in family parties of up to a dozen. Cheetahs and leopards may hunt in pairs. But tigers are usually alone. They patrol an area of forest and hunt by stealth — waiting for prey to appear, creeping up on it, and pouncing. Most of their food consists of small mammals and birds.

This tiger probably slept through the heat of the day, waking in the evening feeling empty, hungry, and restless for action. She has walked quietly for two or three hours along miles of forest track, with one or two cubs trotting and running behind her. She has stopped repeatedly to sniff the air, stooping to investigate new scents along the track, calling quietly to keep her cubs in order. Now she has stopped again, ears and tail twitching. Something has caught her attention, perhaps a wild pig blundering over the forest floor, or an antelope treading silently. Whatever it is, it is coming toward her.

She lies in wait on a rocky mound. She waits — and waits — until it comes within reach. Then she leaps. It will be a lucky pig or antelope that escapes those bared teeth and extended claws and the massive weight of her muscular body. The cubs gather round. Their mother has not taught, but they have learned, and now the family can enjoy the feast.

Shark STEALTHY HUNTER OF THE OCEANS

There are many different kinds of sharks, most of them less than 3 ft (1 m) long and harmless to people. Just a few kinds grow bigger than that – big enough to hunt game fish, dolphins and whales. Here a big blue shark, about 10 ft (3 m) long, has caught up with a tuna just over half its length, hit it hard enough to stun the fish, and bitten a piece from its flank. The shark will turn around and make another attack, this time holding and shaking until the tuna dies from shock and loss of blood.

Sharks and tuna are both small-brained fish. Tuna are fast-moving, agile, and very efficient at catching smaller fish. How can a shark outsmart a tuna? It is not just speed or agility that counts. Sharks find their prey from far away by detecting scents and vibrations in the water. They swim fast and know, by instinct or learning, how to approach and use their strength against different kinds of prey. Tuna can keep out of a shark's way most of the time. This tuna may have been sick, or old, or just for a moment not paying attention to danger. That first hit and bite by the shark made the tuna almost helpless. It will be very lucky to escape.

Sharks have wide jaws with several rows of very sharp teeth that are being replaced all the time. They are often hungry and always ready to bite.

Kingfisher FLASH OF BLUE OVER THE STREAM

Walk quietly by a clear, flowing stream and you may be lucky enough to see one of these beautiful birds — a kingfisher. There are over eighty different kinds, and they live throughout the world. Nearly all kingfishers have long bills, short tails, and brilliant colors in their plumage.

This is the common kingfisher that you see all over Europe and North Africa and across Asia to China and Japan. Wherever it lives, it finds a stretch of riverbank that becomes its home. Winter and summer alike, it patrols constantly, with rapid, darting flight, to find out where the fish are hiding. Often you will see it perched on a stump of willow or an alder branch, preening, looking about, and peering into the water. Watch closely. Again, if you are lucky, you may see it dive off the perch and disappear with a splash into the stream.

To a fish in the stream, it looks much like this. These minnows have heard and felt the violent splash, and turned with a flick of the tail to escape. They may see the brilliant colors and bubbles, but for one of them it is too late to get away. The kingfisher can swim, pushing and steering itself through the water with half-folded wings. The long, pointed bill darts left and right, and one of the two minnows is taken.

Returning to its perch, the kingfisher shakes the water from its feathers, throws the fish into the air, catches it headfirst, and swallows it whole. One small minnow does not last very long, so within minutes ithe kingfisher is ready to hunt again.

The kingfisher returns to its perch, and in a moment it will throw the fish into the air and catch it headfirst, so that it can be swallowed more easily.

Anaconda SILENT STRANGLER

The snake is an anaconda, or water boa, about 10 ft (3 m) long and possibly 1 ft (30 cm) in diameter. Its prey is a South American marsh deer, the size of a small dog. Both live in the marshes close to the River Amazon, in Brazil.

Anacondas do not feed every day or even every week. When hungry, they lie in wait, often at the edge of a stream or marsh, sometimes draping themselves from a tree overhanging a path. Any small animal that comes along is likely to be attacked. The anaconda strikes with its mouth, holds on, and coils its body like a spring around its prey. As the prey struggles, the anaconda contracts its muscles to tighten the "spring." After a few minutes, the animal cannot breathe and dies of suffocation.

Then a remarkable thing happens. The anaconda unwinds, opens its jaws wide, and begins to swallow the prey. If the creature is wider than the anaconda, this takes time, but starting at the narrowest point (usually the muzzle), the snake slides its mouth over the animal, if necessary unhinging its jaws to widen the gape. First the head disappears, then the rest of the body, inch by inch. An anaconda that has just eaten heartily looks like a suitcase with a head at one end and a tail at the other. It slides off to a quiet corner of the marsh and may spend several weeks digesting its meal.

Has this anaconda killed a deer too big for it to swallow? It will try its best and may well succeed.

Freshwater pike TERROR OF THE DUCK POND

Here is a big fish with big silvery eyes and a very big mouth, just about to grab a mallard duckling. Pike make their living by lying very still at the bottom of a pond or stream. They like clear water, so they can see what is going on around them. They watch for movement, which they also feel through their sensitive skin. An insect larva, a small fish, even a snail crawling slowly along the bottom of the pond is enough to gain their attention. A quick flurry of movement, a snap of those monstrous jaws, and the pike settles back to watch for its next meal.

Pike can see upward as well as sideways, and a duckling paddling overhead on the surface of the stream makes a lot of ripples. This duckling hatched from an egg only a few days ago, in a nest at the side of the stream, along with seven or eight others. When only a few hours old, as soon as they could stand and walk, the chicks were led by the mother mallard to the water to swim and feed. She could not warn them of all the dangers around, but her constant, gentle quacking kept them in the safest place, close by her body.

This duckling got lost, left behind for a few moments when the family group moved on. The pike has seen it, and with a powerful swish of the tail, sweeps through the water toward it. The duckling has not seen it and will never know what came up from below to grab and swallow it down.

Pike may become so large — growing to weights of more than 50 lb (22.5 kg) — and aggressive that they will attack and eat smaller ones, sometimes with fatal results for themselves.

African hunting dogs KILLERS ON THE LOOSE

If you saw dogs like these wandering around town, you might well recognize them as dogs, but you would want to keep out of their way. They are rough-haired, with big rounded ears, long noses, and long legs for running. Here they are running down a Burchell's zebra on a dusty African plain.

Zebras are close kin to horses, white but covered with black stripes. They live in herds, eating grass and defending themselves by kicking and biting. One zebra could probably see off one hunting dog without any trouble. But hunting dogs seldom live alone. They gather in extended family groups or packs, which together can hunt animals much bigger and stronger than themselves. When stalking zebras, they advance slowly toward them, set the herd running, and look for the one that is weakest, lame, or quick to tire.

Even a tired zebra can kick hard with its hooves or bite with those blunt teeth. But three or four dogs between them can bring it down and kill it, and the zebra provides a good meal for the whole pack.

Index PREDATORS, PREY, AND PLACES

A
Africa 6, 8, 12, 32, 40, 46
African hunting dogs 46-47
Amazon, River 42
anaconda 42-43
antlers 28
Asia 40

B
barn owl 10-11
bat 30-31
bear 16-17
Bengal tiger 36-37
bill 11, 26, 40
bird-eating spider 24-25
bite 24, 34, 46
blue shark 38-39
Brazil 42
buffalo 8

C
Canada 28
carcass 14
cheetah 6-7, 13, 36
China 40
claws 11, 16, 18, 36
crocodile 32-33

D
dogs 46-47

E
ears 30
energy 6
Europe 40

F
fangs 35
fish 38, 44-45
forests 16, 18, 28, 36

G
gentoo penguin 14-15
grizzly bear 16-17

H
heron 26-27
hooves 8, 46
horns 8
humans, see man
hyenas 12-13

I
Indonesia 18

J
Japan 40
jaws 14, 20, 32, 34, 42

K
kicking 46
kingfisher 40-41
Komodo dragon 18-19

L
leopard 36
leopard seal 14-15
lions 8-9, 13, 36
lizard 18
long-eared bat 30-31

M
mallard duck 44
man/human 7, 25, 38
mantis 20-21
mongoose 34-35
mouth 42

N
North America 16
nutrients 6

O
oceans 38
owl 10-11

P
pack 12, 46
penguins 14-15
pike 44-45
pincers 20
poison 24, 25, 35
praying mantis 20-21
prey 6, 7
  antelopes 12, 32-33, 36
  beetles 30
  birds 10, 14, 16, 24, 36
  buffalo 8-9
  Burchell's zebra 46
  caribou 28-29
  cobra 34-35
  deer 42-43
  duckling 44-45
  eggs 16, 24
  fish 16, 26-27, 40, 44
  giraffes 12
  grasshopper 20
  insects 10, 30
  larvae 44
  locust 20
  macaque 18
  mammals 36
  mice 10, 16
  minnows 40
  monkeys 18
  moths 30
  penguins 14-15
  rabbits 10, 22-23
  roach 26
  salmon 16
  snail 44
  snake 34-35
  springbok 32
  squirrels 16
  tuna 38-39
  voles 10
  whales 38
  wild pig 36
  zebras 12, 46-47
pride (of lions) 8

R
reptiles 18
riverbank 40

S
savanna 6, 8
seal 14-15
shark 38-39
sleep 16
snake 42-43
South America 42
Southern Ocean 14
spider 24-25
stoat 22-23

T
talons 10, 11
teeth 22, 32, 35, 36, 38
tiger 36-37
timber wolves 28-29

W
water boa 42
wolves 28-29